Grammaropolis PRESENTS

Li'l Pete the Preposition

Written by Coert Voorhees

Illustrations by Powerhouse Animation

Meet the Parts of Speech

I name a specific person, place, thing, or idea. It's a big responsibility, naming things—a responsibility that requires a certain attention to detail.

Nelson the Noun

Some people say I'm all over the place. Some people call me a ball of energy. I take that as a compliment, because I just like to go, go, go!

Vinny the Action Verb

I take the place of one or more Nouns or Pronouns. I always want the Noun's job, and I hang out with the Verb and Adjective.

Roger the Pronoun

I'm perfectly happy to link Nouns and Pronouns with the appropriate Adjectives, but it's not like I'm going to expend a lot of energy doing so.

Lucy the Linking Verb

I modify a Noun or Pronoun. I tell what kind, which one, how many, or how much. I pride myself on being the most artistic of the parts of speech.

Jake the Adjective

Gather 'round everybody and let's have ourselves a wonderful time. I just love bringing words and groups of words together, don't you?

Connie the Conjunction

I modify a Verb, Adjective, or other Adverb. I tell how, when, where, to what extent, and under what condition. I often end in –ly, but I don't have to.

Benny the Adverb

I express emotion!! Yep, I'm always here, always ready with my commas and exclamation points, just in case.

Izzy the Interjection

They call me Preposition because I'm pre-positioned. I'm first. At the front. Before every other word in the phrase? Got it?

Li'l Pete the Preposition

I am a chameleon. A spy. An undercover operative. I infiltrate the sentence and act as whatever part of speech suits me.

Slang

LI'L PETE THE PREPOSITION

© 2019 Grammaropolis

Graphic Design by Mckee Frazior

Text and Illustrations © 2011 by Grammaropolis LLC

This book is typeset in Komika Text

Distributed throughout the world by Ingram Publisher Services www.ingrambook.com

Li'l Pete's job was to connect a noun or a pronoun to another word in the sentence.

The noun or pronoun he connected was called the "object of the preposition."

Merit Badge
Use STREET as the object.

And because he was the preposition, he came at the beginning of the phrase.

eing a preposition was a big responsibility, and Li'l Pete was
roud of it.

Although sometimes he let it get to his head.

i'l Pete had to determine the very best prepositional phrases o control his model rocket.

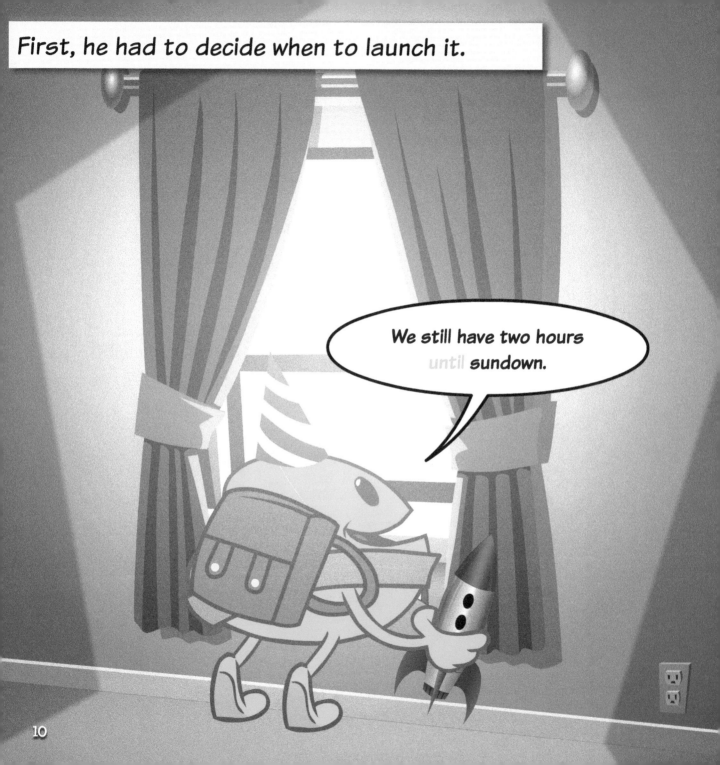

According to his mom, inside the house wasn't a good launching spot.

e had to figure out where else to launch the rocket, so he
sed prepositions that located an object in space.

Finally, he had to figure out the logical relationship between his objects and the rest of the sentence.

I'll launch it like a pro. People will love me for being awesome!

even used compound prepositions, which were made of
re than one word.

But then Li'l Pete got so excited that he forgot to add objects to his prepositions.

Fly around! Go between! Zoom on!

And that turned some of them into adverbs.

ithout the objects, the prepositions didn't show any lation to anything.

Li'l Pete had no control over the rocket.

Luckily, his friends reminded him what was missing.

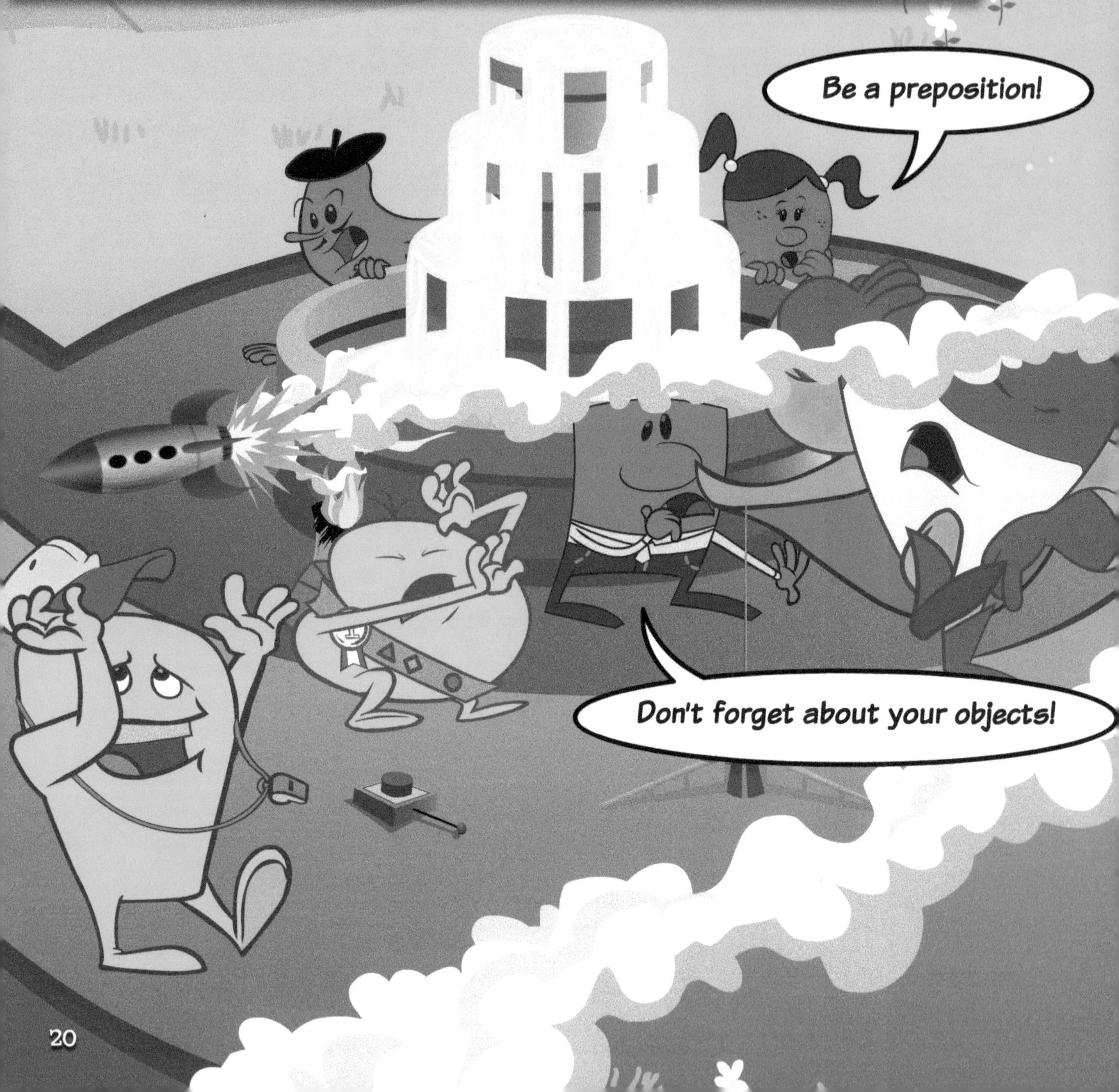

PREPOSITIONS

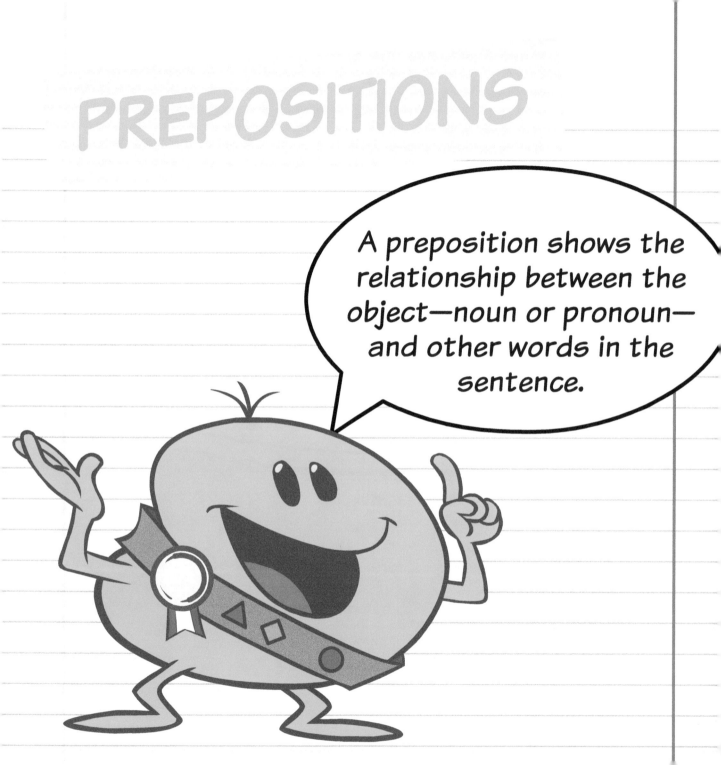

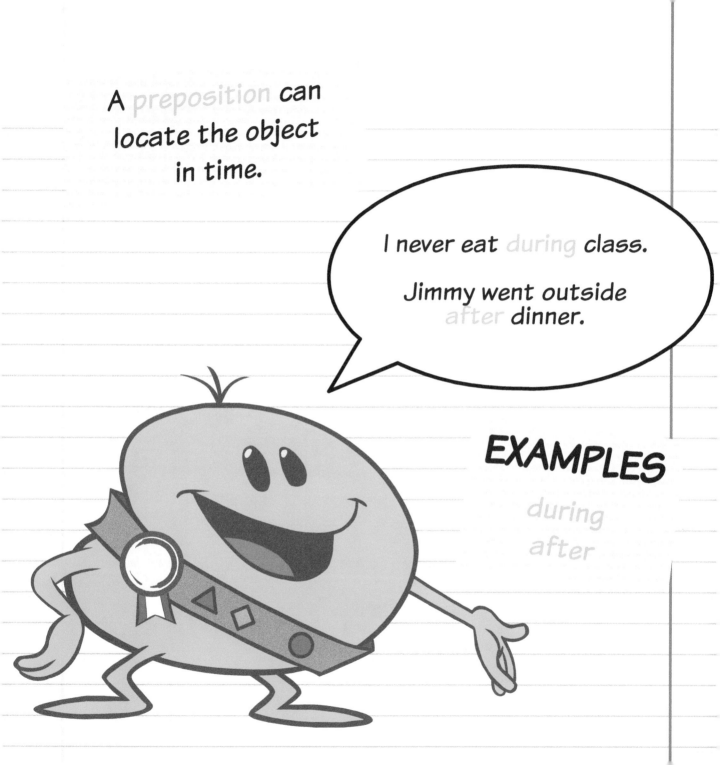

A *preposition* can locate the object in the space.

The moon shone brightly *in* the night sky.

I left a key *under* the welcome mat.

EXAMPLES

in

under

A *preposition* can show a logical relationship between the object and another word in the sentence.

I have always wanted to dance *like* Ginger.

Are people still looking *for* the fountain *of* youth?

EXAMPLES

like
for
of

COMPOUND PREPOSITIONS

A compound preposition is a single preposition that is more than one word.

We won the game because of Billy's lucky shoes.

According to my dad, the meteor shower is over.

EXAMPLES

because of

According to

PREPOSITIONS & ADVERBS

Some words can be used as either prepositions or adverbs, but how do you tell the difference? Remember that a preposition always has to be at the front of the phrase. If there's no phrase, it's not a preposition!

PREPOSITION

We ran around the field.

around the field is a prepositional phrase, so around is a preposition.

ADVERB

We ran around.

around is by itself, without the rest of a phrase. That means it's an adverb.

CPSIA information can be obtained
at www.ICGtesting.com
Printed in the USA
BVHW020504110519
547997BV00002B/5/P